MANCHESTER FROM THE AIR

MANCHESTER FROM THE AIR

WEBBAVIATION.CO.UK

breedon books
PUBLISHING

First published in Great Britain in 2007 by

The Breedon Books Publishing Company Limited

Breedon House, 3 The Parker Centre,

Derby, DE21 4SZ.

ISBN 978-1-85983-557-9

Printed and bound in China

Acknowledgements

There are many people who have helped in the making of this book, and I would like to express particular thanks to the following: John Seville, the UK's best photo pilot whose skill in placing the aircraft precisely where required must be telepathic; the long suffering National Air Traffic Control Service at Manchester airport, who are always helpful in squeezing a photo detail between the airliners; fellow aerial photographers Catherine Wheildon and William Cross for their friendship, support and stress counselling.

Contents

Introduction

Manchester is a fascinating city and is currently undergoing a boom, the likes of which it has not experienced since it pioneered the Industrial Revolution. The subjects I have photographed range from the Roman fort at Castlefield to the very latest cutting-edge architecture such as the Imperial War Museum at Salford Quays and the Beetham Tower. The area is a lively, modern urban conurbation but still contains historical gems from the distant past, such as the 15th-century buildings at the Chetham's School of Music. In choosing the geographical boundaries of this book, I have decided to ignore the political divisions and simply choose the boundary most visible from the air, the M60 ring road. Thus the subjects include Manchester, Salford and the suburbs up to and including the ring road. It is an interesting historical fact that, although Manchester has tended to dominate in recent years, in previous centuries it was Salford that was the major town. In the last six years, though, Salford is starting to catch up, and the Quays area is a model for regenerating an area.

Pages 8 and 9: Barton Aerodrome with the city centre in the background, Britain's first municipal airport, and the location of the world's oldest operational control tower and the base for most of my flying.

Suburban

Ancoats

Typical Manchester, terraced housing, so evocative of the Ancoats area, which was the world's first industrial suburb. This area was known as little Italy due to the large number of Italian immigrants in the 19th century. It is now a conservation area and is being extensively redeveloped, and thanks to local preservation groups many of the fine 18th and 19th-century buildings, such as St Peter's Church and Murrays' Mill complex, are being restored and given new uses. Prominent in the photograph is the *Daily Express* building: one of Manchester's most striking buildings, with its black glass, 1930s art-deco architecture.

Pages 12 and 13: Platt Fields Park and Fallowfield with Wilbraham Road in the foreground, looking across Moss Side towards the city centre.

Ardwick

In recent years Manchester has had a great deal of regeneration, with large parts of the city being reconstructed. These images show the Grove Village project. The estate is being remodelled with new housing, three neighbourhood parks and a new village centre to provide modern urban living. The work has involved the demolition of over 400 houses and construction of over 600 new houses, together with the refurbishment of another 600 houses. The remodelled layout features a new 'Green Route' through the estate, to provide a green and safe route, with traffic calming and recreational areas.

East Manchester

From above, Manchester is a very green city, as this view clearly shows. Taken from over Failsworth, looking west over Newton Heath towards the city centre, you can see the surprising number of trees, particularly along the Medlock River valley at Clayton Vale on the left of the photograph. Clayton Vale is a designated 'Site of Biological Importance', and it is popular with walkers and nature lovers.

Moss Side

Above: Alexandra Park was opened in 1870 and was one of the first public parks in the city. The oval on the right was originally constructed to house a cricket pitch, and then later a bandstand was built. The dry ground of summer shows up a circle in the grass, in the centre of which used to be the bandstand.

Right: Maine Road, Moss Side. Once home to the Manchester City football stadium, all that now remains is the outline of the stadium, while its replacement can be seen in the background at the top of the photograph. The area is about to be redeveloped with new houses.

Platt Fields Park

Platt Fields Park was originally a private estate but was later bought and redeveloped by Manchester Corporation and opened as a public park on 7 May 1910. Its main feature, the man-made lake, measures over six acres and can be seen for a considerable distance from the air. The park has been a popular venue for a variety of events over the years, including the Manchester Flower Show.

Prestwich

This page: A parade marches down Bury New Road in Prestwich, while the fun fair is in full swing in St Mary's Park below.

Right: St Mary's Church, Prestwich, has been a church site for over 800 years, with parts of the current church being constructed at various periods and much of it dating from the 15th and 16th centuries.

Princess Road

Princess Road at its intersection with Platt Lane, Fallowfield. After World War Two, large parts of Manchester were rebuilt to replace bomb-damaged and slum housing. These new council estates were intended to provide quality housing for working people and have proved much more successful than the high-rise experiments of the 1960s and 70s.

Salford

Broad Street, one of the main road arteries into Salford and Manchester city centre, and the flats on Cannon Street. The City of Salford is often overshadowed by Manchester, but historically it was Salford that was the key town, with Manchester being just a part of what was once called Salfordshire, which covered most of what is now Greater Manchester. The area is now thriving with the regenerated Salford Quays and a strong student population attending the university there.

St Marys and Whitworth Park

Above: St Mary's Hospital for Women and Children was founded in 1790 and today is still a key asset within the Central Manchester Healthcare Trust. It is also part of a £250 million reconstruction project.

Right: Whitworth Park was built as a memorial to Sir Joseph Whitworth, the engineer, and was opened in 1890. In the top corner of the park is the Whitworth Art Gallery, which is part of the University of Manchester and is famous for its collection of textiles and wallpapers.

Stretford

Left: Looking south east towards Manchester Airport, this view shows the green 'urban countryside' of the Mersey valley, with the M60 motorway winding its way towards Stockport. Note the Bridgewater Canal, which was built by the Duke of Bridgewater to transport coal. Today it is a leisure recourse, bringing holidaymakers into the heart of the city. Here you can see the canal running through Stretford and onwards, under the motorway, to Sale on its way to Runcorn. Alongside the canal is the Metrolink line, taking busy commuters to work: the old and the new side by side.

Above: Looking east across Stretford towards Whalley Range and Chorlton-cum-Hardy.

Pages 34 and 35: Looking north along Chester Road towards the city centre.

Whalley Range

Above: In the foreground running left to right is Withington Road, with College Road running top to bottom past the now empty GMB College, where a generation of Union activists were trained. Whalley Range was one of the first well-to-do suburbs of Manchester to appear after the city expanded during the Industrial Revolution. The area was laid out by Victorian property developer Samuel Brookes according to his vision, and many of the original 19th-century buildings remain. There is currently a booming property market, and to halt the loss of many of the larger houses the area was made a conservation area in 1991.

Right: A close up of the area between Withington Road and Alexandra Road South, with the renaissance style St Bede's College at the top right.

Education

The University of Manchester

Manchester University, with over 35,000 students, is one of the largest in the UK. Formerly called the Victoria University of Manchester, it was merged with the University of Manchester Institute of Science and Technology (UMIST) in 2004. Ernest Rutherford began his research here, leading to the splitting of the atom, and it was here that the world's first programmable computer was built in 1948 by Tom Kilburn and Sir Freddie Williams. Twenty Nobel prize winners have studied or worked at the university.

Pages 38 and 39: Salford University.

Above: Manchester Metropolitan University.
Left: The North Campus, formerly UMIST.

Salford University

The University of Salford can trace its roots back to 1896, when the Salford Working Men's College merged with the Pendleton Mechanics Institute to form the Salford Technical Institute. The original courses of mathematics, engineering, physics, building, chemistry, dyeing, spinning and weaving, and art reflected the industrialisation of 19th-century Salford and Manchester. The University has over 18,000 students and more than 2,500 staff and is currently undergoing a £130 million program of construction and upgrading, including new buildings for the faculty of health and social care and a flagship new centre for arts and media students.

Chetham's School of Music

The famous Chetham's School of Music is the largest specialist music school in the UK and resides in a remarkable collection of buildings, dating back to mediaeval times. The school was established in 1969 on the site of the Chetham's Hospital. The buildings to the right of the photograph, which include the Baronial Hall and Cloisters, were constructed in the 15th century. Chetham's Library has been collecting works since the mid-17th century. The large building in the centre of the image was originally built for the Manchester Grammar School in the late 19th century. The small building towards the top of the image is the Vallins Art Centre, designed by architect Alfred Waterhouse, who also designed the Town Hall, University Quadrangle and nearby Strangeways Prison.

Architecture

Beetham Tower

Beetham Tower is the tallest mixed-use building in the United Kingdom and is the highest residential building in Western Europe. Designed by architect Ian Simpson, at 171 metres and 48 storeys it is the UK's tallest building outside of London. The tower includes 219 apartments and a five-star hotel and is notable for its extremely slender design. The upper residential portion of the tower is marked by a step where the upper floors are built out four metres wider than the lower floors. Another feature is the 'Blade' on the roof, which is intended to visually blend the building into the sky.

Pages 46 and 47: Piccadilly
Pages 50 and 51: Beetham Tower

Fish Market

Above: The old Fish Market in Manchester's Northern Quarter lost its roof long ago, and now only the outer walls of the original building remain. The site has now been redeveloped to provide mixed urban living space and commercial use with new buildings inside the preserved and listed original perimeter wall.

Bridgewater Hall

The concert hall, designed by RHWL Architects, upended in 1996 and is noted not just for its stunning architecture but also its excellent acoustics. The hall is home to both the Hallé and BBC Philharmonic Orchestras and also hosts a wide variety of performances from jazz to pop. In 1998 it won the Civic Trust Special Award for the new building that has done the most to enhance the appearance of a city centre.

CIS Building

When opened in 1962, the CIS building was the third-tallest in Europe and remained the tallest in the UK outside London for 40 years. The concrete service section of the tower was recently re-clad in Solar panels to make this one of Manchester's greenest buildings.

Portland Tower

Also completed in 1962, the Portland Tower was designed by Leach Rhodes Walker. The tower is 80 metres high and has some 21 floors; however, this is now dwarfed by the current crop of skyscrapers such as the Beetham Tower and the proposed 188-metre, 60-storey Inacity Tower.

The Midland Hotel

Above: The hotel is famous as the place where Mr Rolls met Mr Royce, leading to the formation of the Rolls-Royce motor company. It was designed by Charles Trubshaw for the Midland Railway Company and completed in 1903. It offers 303 bedrooms and 14 luxury suites with two restaurants, including the double AA rosette award-winning French restaurant.

Crown Court

Left: The grade II listed, Gothic-revival style Crown Court on Minshull Street was built from 1867 to 1873 to a design by Thomas Worthington. The building has recently been upgraded by Hurd Rolland Architects with new courts and a glazed atrium over the old courtyard to link all the courts together.

GMEX

Built in 1880 as Manchester's Central Station by the Cheshire Lines railway, the station served the LNER, LMS and later British Rail until the trains finally ceased to run in May 1969. The 200ft-wide glass roof originally covered six platforms and nine railway tracks. Following a tragic period as a car park, the site was then transformed into the GMEX exhibition centre. Now the single-span roof provides an undivided 7,500sq m exhibition space, which is also used as a concert and sporting venue. Adjacent and connected to it is the new Manchester International Convention Centre.

The Great Northern Railway Company's Goods Warehouse

The grade II listed Great Northern Warehouse was built in 1899 by a team of 800 men to a design by W.T. Foxlee. It employed 350 men and offered a next-day delivery service to any station in Britain. The warehouse was built over the top of the underground Manchester and Salford Junction Canal, which had been cut in two by the building of Central Station. However, shafts were sunk beneath the warehouse, and the canal was then reused for barge loading and unloading. The canal became disused in 1922, but during World War Two it was drained and used as an air-raid shelter. Today the underground canal is still there and is a piece of Manchester that remains hidden. The warehouse itself became disused in 1963 but was then rebuilt to offer shops, bars, cafés and car parking.

MEN Arena

The Manchester Evening News Arena, opened in 1995, is Europe's largest indoor concert venue. Originally built with the 2000 Olympics bid in mind, it has since proved a huge success for holding concerts and events, with more than a million people visiting during its first year alone. In 2001 it won the Pollstar award for 'International Venue of the Year', and in 2003–04 it won the world's busiest arena venue, based on concert-ticket sales. A series of concerts by the band Take That were seen by 140,000 people and 84,000 came to see Kylie Minogue. Other events include concerts by Madonna, Sir Paul McCartney, Pavarotti and The Rolling Stones. Sporting events have included football, ice hockey and boxing, and it was used in the 2002 Commonwealth Games.

Manchester Evening News

The *Manchester Evening News* has recently signed up for this brand new office in the Spinningfields development. The newspaper was started as an election sheet in 1868, by prospective MP Mitchell Henry. After the election, it was taken over by Peter Allen and John Edward Taylor, who developed it, and it continued to grow until, by 1939, it was the largest regional newspaper in Britain. Today it continues to develop, now owning the *Metro News*, Britain's widest-circulating free newspaper, and working on new multimedia ventures including a Manchester TV channel.

Victoria Baths

Victoria Baths was opened on 7 September 1906. Designed by Henry Price, who was Manchester's first city architect, the baths included three pools, a laundry and a Turkish bath. No expense was spared on the building, which was beautifully clad in brick and terracotta on the outside and ceramic tiles on the inside with stained-glass windows. In 1952 Britain's first public jacuzzi was installed. However, the baths then fell into decline and were closed in 1993. Since then there has been a strong campaign to restore the building to its former glory, and after winning BBC2's *Restoration* it looks well on the way to success.

Oxford Road

Here we see the junction of Whitworth Street West and Oxford Road, with the trendy new apartments on the corner contrasting with the apparently tiny Ritz dance hall next door. On the right and in the close up photograph we can see the Baroque Portland Stone façade of the grade II listed St James Building by Clegg, Fryer & Penman from 1912, originally commissioned by the Calico Printers' Association and now home to numerous businesses. An interesting survivor of times gone by is the tiny yellow Peveril of the Peak pub in the upper right of the image. On the station approach is the famous Cornerhouse Cinema and Art Gallery.

Piccadilly Gardens

Recently remodelled, the gardens feature a walk through an interactive fountain and a café pavilion by Japanese architect Tadao Ando, designed to shield the gardens from the hubbub of the neighbouring transport interchange. Although entirely renewed, the gardens still contain one link with the past: the 1901 Queen Victoria memorial by Edward Onslow Ford.

Royal Exchange

Above: Originally built as a cotton exchange, the Royal Exchange now contains shops and the Royal Exchange Theatre, which was founded by a group of artistic directors in 1968. As well as traditional works, the theatre is strongly supportive of new works.

Palace Hotel

Right: Originally the Refuge Assurance building, it was converted to a hotel in 1996. The building is another work by Sir Alfred Waterhouse and his son Paul. Opened in 1910, the brick and terracotta building is grade II listed.

Chorlton Street

Above: At the bottom of the image we can see MMUBS, the Manchester Metropolitan University Business School, and running up the centre of the image towards Portland Tower is Chorlton Street in the heart of the nightlife area with its cafés and bars. Slightly to the left is Sackville Park, notable as the location of the statue of Alan Turing, the computer pioneer.

Manchester Metropolitan University Hollings Campus – the toast-rack

Left: Known locally as 'the toast-rack' the Hollings College was designed by L.C. Howitt and opened in 1960. The adjoining circular building is known as the fried egg. The buildings were grade II listed in 1998. Originally a catering college, it now caters for fashion as well as food.

Manchester Town Hall

Opened in 1887, the Gothic revival town hall was Alfred Waterhouse's masterpiece. It cost a million pounds to build and was lavishly decorated with statues and carvings of important Mancunian figures, including General Agricola, the founder of the original Roman fort of Mamuciam. The town hall is notable for its 85m-tall clock tower and also a series of 12 frescoes by Ford Madox Brown. In front of the town hall is Albert Square, and prominent in the photograph is the memorial to Prince Albert of Saxe-Coburg and Gotha, who would no doubt feel very at home during the regular German markets held in the square.

URBIS

Situated in Cathedral Gardens, central Manchester Urbis offers a 'dynamic programme of changing exhibitions offering unique insights into the culture of the modern city, with innovative explorations of design, architecture, graffiti, music and the urban environment'. It is also home to Channel M, the Manchester TV channel. The building, opened in 2002, was designed by Ian Simpson and cost £30 million.

Pages 78 and 79: Urbis and the triangle.

Commerce

Canal Street

Above: Along the bank of the Rochdale Canal lies Canal Street. Once an area of derelict warehouses, it has now been transformed into a centrepiece of trendy cafés, bars and clubs. The Rochdale Canal was opened in 1804 to connect the Bridgewater Canal with Rochdale and beyond as far as Sowerby Bridge. The canal fell into disuse in the 20th century, most being closed in 1952, but it is now being restored, and in 2002 the canal was again fully navigable.

Mosley Street

Left: The heart of the financial district, the area in and around Mosley Street contains some wonderful architectural gems, such as the Portico Library (1806), the Bradford and Bingley building, the Royal Bank of Scotland (1862), the Midland bank (1935), designed by Sir Edwin Lutyens, on Kings Street and the wonderfully Baroque Parrs Bank (1902).

Trafford Park

Trafford Park is the world's first and biggest industrial park, created in 1896 when the De Trafford family sold the estate to Trafford Park Estates. Originally a park, the location adjacent to the Manchester Ship Canal made it ideal for industrial development, and although the docks have now closed the adjacent motorways link the park with the modern transport system. Many famous names have moved here, including Hovis in 1914, Kellogs in 1938 and the Westinghouse Electric company (later Metropolitan Vickers) in 1899. My grandfather built Model T Fords here, and it was here that a Mr Allcock met a Mr Brown at the Vickers plant to plan the first transatlantic flight in 1919.

The Northern Quarter

Mancunians have always had a strong entrepreneurial spirit, and this shows strongly today in the city's Northern Quarter, with its multitude of small businesses. The area has not had the same level of renewal as other parts of the city, but this has allowed the area to retain its own individual character, a character of small and medium businesses often catering for more unusual niche markets. There are some 610 businesses in the M4 area with a strong presence from creative businesses such as designers, architects and marketing firms.

Retail

The Arndale Centre

When completed in 1979, the Manchester Arndale Centre, with over 200 shops, was Europe's largest enclosed shopping centre. The centre was designed by architects Hugh Wilson and Lewis Womersley and has recently been modernised with a new glass and steel entrance to Exchange Square and a new glass-roofed Winter Garden.

The Big Wheel

With 42 carriages, lit by 51,000 bulbs and 60 metres high, this big wheel is one of the largest mobile big wheels in the world. It was first seen at Champs Elysees, Paris, for the millennium, where it sported a special leather-trimmed VIP carriage for President Jacques Chirac. One of a number built by Nauta-Bussink in the Netherlands, the wheel was brought to Manchester as a temporary attraction for the Christmas 2004 period. The wheel needs no permanent fixtures as it is ballasted by tanks containing 40,000 litres of water. A new wheel was brought back for Christmas 2005–06 and dismantled in the spring of 2006 ready for its next outing in the beautiful city of Dresden, Germany, although it is likely to come back to Manchester again in the near future.

The Triangle

Formerly the Corn Exchange, the Triangle, built between 1897 and 1903, has recently been remodelled with major structural alterations to the interior, including a new feature staircase, to provide a first-class shopping arcade. There had been a produce market on the site since mediaeval times, and the design by architects Ball and Else is notable for its iron and glass-domed roof and the new giant TV screen on its exterior wall. The building lies within the Cathedral Conservation Area, created in 1972.

Stretford Shopping Centre

Above: The former Stretford Arndale centre was built as one of a string of 18 Arndale shopping centres around the UK. Set up by Arnold Hagenbach and Sam Chippindale, after whom they were named, these were the country's first American mall-style shopping centres.

M&S

Left: It was in Manchester that Marks and Spencer set up their first store, and today, not far from their original Cheetham site, is their new flagship store. The store has been built from scratch, involving the demolition of the previous nine-storey building. It is the largest M&S store in the world, with over 23,500sq m of floorspace. Designed by Building Design Partnership and built by Bovis, the new structure is walled in glass with a glass tube walkway connecting it to the adjacent Arndale Centre.

Pages 98 and 99: The Trafford Centre.

Sport

Sport in Manchester

Manchester has always had a strong sporting tradition from grass-roots up to the very top levels of sports. The city has a whole host of sporting facilities, including two top football teams, the National Squash Centre and the Manchester Aquatics Centre. The City hosted the 2002 Commonwealth Games, for which many of these facilities were constructed. Above is Woodhouses Cricket Club and right is the Power League Five-a-Side Soccer Centre in Ardwick.

Manchester Velodrome

Above: Home to the British Cycling Team, the Manchester Velodrome is the National Cycling Centre and Britain's best indoor Olympic cycle track. Purpose-built for the 2002 Commonwealth Games, the centre is one of the world's fastest and the World Track Championships were held here in 1996 and 2000.

The XVII Commonwealth Games

Left: The 2002 Commonwealth Games was the biggest multi-sport event to be held in Britain since the 1948 Olympic Games. The games involved 14 individual and three team sports, with athletes competing from 72 countries. The City of Manchester Stadium was built especially for the event and later reconfigured to serve as home to Manchester City Football Club.

Old Trafford Cricket Ground

Established in 1857, and hosting Test Matches since 1884, this is the home of the Lancashire County Cricket Club and has a capacity of 22,000. Highlights include when Jim Laker was the first to take all 10 wickets in the Test Match against Australia in 1956 and the 1999 World Cup when India played Pakistan to a packed venue. The ground has also hosted non-cricket events such as music concerts.

Trafford Water Sport Centre
Situated in the south of Manchester, the 45-acre lake is used for sailing, angling, windsurfing, kayaking powerboating and model boating. The centre was opened in 1980 using the lake created by extracting gravel to build the adjacent M60 motorway in 1972. The lake and surrounding Mersey Valley are home to a great variety of wildlife and there is a visitors' centre just visible in the top right of the photograph.

The City of Manchester Stadium

Designed by Arup and built by Laing for the Commonwealth Games in 2002, at a cost of £110 million, the stadium was then reconfigured for football by lowering the pitch 10 metres and adding a lower level of seating. The Northern Stand was also completed and roofed over. The stadium has a capacity of 47,000 for football and even more when it is used for concerts. The area around the stadium is known as Sportcity, which includes the adjacent Regional Athletics Arena and National Squash Centre and the Velodrome, in the background of the view above.

Old Trafford

Manchester's most famous building, and probably the world's most famous football club Manchester United, was started in 1878 as the Newton Heath, Lancashire and Yorkshire Railway football club. The Old Trafford stadium, also known as the 'Theatre of Dreams', has been the home of the club since 1910, and with a capacity of 76,000 it is the second largest stadium in Britain after the new Wembley Stadium. In 2006 the North Stand corners were filled in to add 9,000 seats. Further enlargement to the south is hindered by the railway line, although the lower roof level of the south side lends itself to aerial photographs of the stadium.

Transport

Piccadilly

The areas around the junction of the Ashton Canal and Rochdale Canal at Piccadilly have seen a lot of changes over the years, from industrial boom in the 18th and 19th centuries to the decline in the late 20th century and now back to boom with the current regeneration. The close up above shows the new Paradise Wharf development, and much of the remaining open space in these images is about to be reconstructed. There are plans for a 188 metre/58-storey tower called Inacity Tower, which will be built on the car park to the right foreground of the image on the left.

Pages 114 and 115: The Bridgewater Canal in the Castlefield conservation area.

Hulme Arch

Above: Princess Road as is passes under the new 25 metre-high Hulme Arch, which carries Stretford Road, suspended by means of ranked spiral steel cables.

Inner ring road

Right: Manchester has two ring roads, the outer is the M60 motorway and the inner can be seen in this view from the south. The section on the right is the Mancunian Way, which was the region's first urban motorway taking traffic from industrial east Manchester to the docks in the west and was opened by Harold Wilson in 1967. Also in the image we can see the extensive transport infrastructure of the city from the River Irwell, the Bridgewater Canal, the Rochdale Canal and the railways, which have been updated with the new metrolink light rail system.

Thomas Telford Basin

Above: The Thomas Telford Basin is part of the Ashton Canal, which opened in 1796 and links Manchester with Ashton-under-Lyne. It also connects to the Huddersfield Narrow and Peak Forest Canals and forms part of the Cheshire ring. The Ashton Canal fell into disrepair in the mid-20th century, but in 1972–74 it was cleared and reopened by a group of 1,000 volunteers and now serves as an important leisure resource.

Merchants Bridge

Left: Not all Manchester's Canal infrastructure dates from the 18th or 19th century: Merchants Bridge was built in 1995 to cross the Bridgewater Canal and link Slate Wharf and Catalan Square in the Castlefield conservation area. This striking Sickle Arch bridge, designed by RHWL, is constructed of tubular steel and was assembled on the canal bank and then lifted into position by a huge crane.

New East Manchester Gateway

Built at a cost of £36.5 million, the New East Manchester Gateway comprises the Gateway Road, the new Metrolink station with unique copper canopy and the 4,000-ton Finback Bridge, which will carry the Oldham/Rochdale Metrolink extension. The gateway forms a bus/road/rail interchange to serve the new Central Park development, which is bringing high technology employment to the area.

Pages 122 and 123: The New East Manchester Gateway.

Pages 126 and 127: Close-up views of the new Metrolink station.

Oxford Road Station

Above: Oxford Road Station is noted for its unusual architecture, which was built to replace the old Victorian buildings in 1960 when the line was upgraded and electrified. The roof was originally constructed with three conoidal laminated wood shells, reminiscent of the Sydney Opera House.

Piccadilly Station

Left: The biggest and the busiest station in Manchester, with 14 platforms, it is also a terminus for the Metrolink Trams. Originally called London Road Station, it was opened in 1842 as the terminus of the Manchester and Birmingham Railway. The station buildings were rebuilt in 1969 and then remodelled again for the 2002 Commonwealth Games. In the background on the right the little-known and short-lived Mayfield Station can just be seen, which was built in 1910 and closed in 1960.

Railway Depot

Opened in May 2006, this new £30 million train maintenance depot was built to service then new fleet of 185 Pennine Class trains entering service with First TransPennine Express. The fleet of 51 Diesel Multiple Unit trains was built by Siemens at a cost of £200 million and are capable of speeds of 100mph.

Victoria Station

The original building was designed by George Stephenson and opened as the Hunts Bank Station in 1844, with just a single platform to serve the Manchester & Leeds Railway. This grew, and by the late 19th century it was one of the biggest stations in Britain. The distinctive Edwardian frontage was built in 1902 and the station has now been integrated into the Metrolink System and also serves as the terminus for the adjacent MEN Arena.

Salford Quays

Opened in 1894 by Queen Victoria, the Manchester Ship Canal was built to link the docks at Salford Quays to the sea. This allowed Manchester to become Britain's third-largest port and helped the industrialisation of the city. By the 1970s, however, many ships were too big for the canal, and the docks closed in 1982. Since then the area has been regenerated and transformed with new infrastructures such as the Metrolink Trams and the cultural icons of the Lowry Gallery and Imperial War Museum North. The Detroit Bridge (right) was originally a railway swing bridge and linked Salford to Trafford, but it was relocated here to provide a footbridge over the Huron and Erie Basins.

Pages 132 and 133: Salford Quays.

Liverpool Road Station

Above: Opened in 1830, this was the world's first passenger Railway Station and formed the terminus for the Liverpool & Manchester Railway, the one which the famous Rainhill trials were held at to select Stephenson's Rocket as the locomotive. In 1844 the station was replaced for passengers by Victoria Station but continued to be used for freight until 1975. It has now been restored to its 1830 condition and forms the basis of the Museum of Science & Industry.

Left: Salford Quays.

Old Trafford Road Bridge

Above: At 1,800 tons this is the heaviest swing bridge in the UK and was recently rebuilt so that it no longer swings, although the control tower remains next to it as a monument to times gone by.

Barton Swing Bridge

Right: One of the wonders of the industrial age, the aqueduct opened in 1893 and was built to carry the Bridgewater Canal over the Ship Canal. It swings open along with the adjacent road swing bridge to allow larger ships to pass up the canal. This is accomplished by hydraulic sealing doors which seal the water in the bridge and at both ends of the canal, allowing the bridge to swing while containing 800 tons of water.

Swinton Interchange

One of the reasons for the success of Manchester has been its excellent transport infrastructure from canals to railways and now motorways and airports. The Swinton interchange forms the junction between the M62 to Liverpool, the M602 to Salford and the city centre and the M60 orbital ring road. The adjacent Barton Bridge was the first bit of the M60 to be opened, but it took another 40 years before the orbital was completed in 2000.

Culture

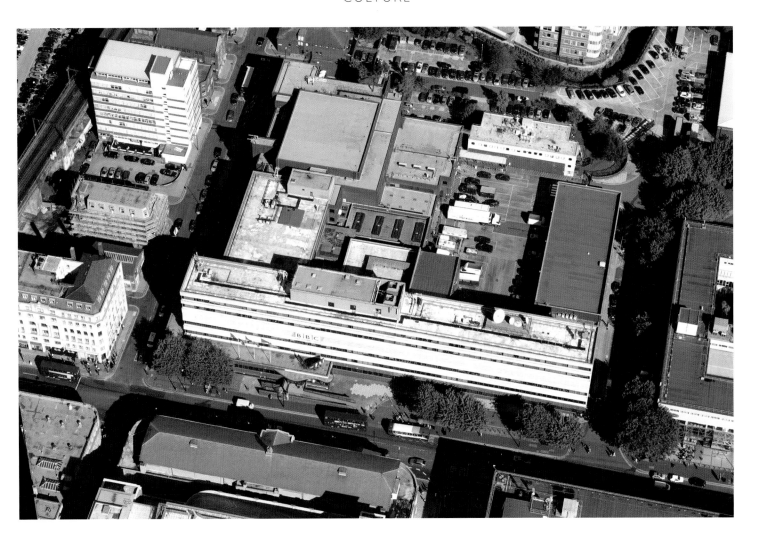

The BBC

Situated on Oxford Road and opened in 1975, the New Broadcasting House produces many local TV programmes and BBC Radio Manchester is broadcast from here via a transmitter on Holme Moss. The future of the building is uncertain at the moment as the BBC is likely to relocate to a new 'Mediacity' at Salford Quays.

The Street

Right in the heart of Manchester are the Granada TV studios, and here we can see the set of its most famous programme *Coronation Street*. Based on a real street in Salford called Archie Street, the first set was indoors and scaled down, but in 1982 this full-sized outdoor version was built, although most of the interior scenes are still shot in the adjoining indoor studio. The neighbouring rows of houses and passing Metrolink tram shown in the programme's opening credits are computer-generated special effects.

Manchester Cathedral

Much of what we see today dates from the 19th century when the cathedral was restored by Joseph Crowther; however, parts of the tower base date back to 1380. The cathedral is sited in the original mediaeval village centre and a St Mary's Church was mentioned in the Domesday book and may well have stood on the same site. In 1421 the church became a Collegiate Foundation, dedicated to St Mary, St Denys and St George, becoming a cathedral in 1847. The church was ransacked during the English Civil War in 1649 and suffered bomb damage during World War Two.

Castlefield Church

Built in 1856 to a design by Edward Walter, the former Congregational Chapel is now a recording studio. To the left of the Congregational Chapel on the wider image the remains of Manchester's first Canal Warehouse, the Grocers Warehouse, can be seen, designed by James Brindley and built in around 1775. Unfortunately it was demolished in 1960.

Castlefield Open Air Theatre

Above: Located in the Giants Basin on the Bridgewater Canal in the Castlefield conservation area, the outdoor arena plays host to a huge variety of events. The canopy is permanently in place allowing impromptu gatherings as well as formal shows. Big screens have also occasionally been set up to show major sporting events such as the 2006 Football World Cup.

Right: Central Library.

Central Library

Following the Public Libraries and Museums Act of 1850, Manchester was the first authority to set up a free lending library in 1852 in the Hall of Science, located where the Science & Industry Museum is now. Construction of a purpose-built library, to a design by E. Vincent Harris, began in 1930 with a foundation laid by Prime Minister Ramsey McDonald. The building has a classical exterior style but was built with a modern steel frame inside and was opened in 1934 by King George V.

The Imperial War Museum North

Opened in 2002 and designed by the world famous architect Daniel Libeskind, the 6,000sq m steel and aluminium building is designed to represent a globe shattered by war into 'shards'. The 'shards' represent the three elements, where war is fought: the main display area is the Earth Shard, the restaurant area is the Water Shard and the tower is the Air Shard. The museum contains exhibits covering various periods of history, with an emphasis on the effect or war on ordinary people.

The Lowry

Opened in 2000, the Lowry spearheaded the regeneration of the Salford Quays area. The gallery houses many works by local artist Laurence Stephen Lowry, after whom the building takes its name. There is a large collection of work by other artists from various styles and periods, as well as two theatres. Designed by Michael Wilford, the building required 48,000 tons of concrete, 5,263sq m of glass and 2,466 tons of steel to build it and, together with the adjacent plaza and lifting footbridge, cost £106 million.

Pages 158 and 159: The Lowry and Salford Quays lifting footbridge.

Manchester Art Gallery

Acquired by the Manchester Corporation in 1882, the gallery has recently had a four-year and £35 million redevelopment, which included an adjoining new building by Michael Hopkins and Partners. The gallery now has 2,500sq m of display space to show the 25,000 items in its collection of fine art, decorative art and costume. With the help of the Contemporary Art Society, the gallery has also acquired a collection of contemporary furniture, sculpture and photography.

The Roman Fort

The Roman General Julius Agricola settled in Manchester in AD 79, building his fort on a hill overlooking the confluence of the Rivers Medlock and Irwell. The Roman name 'Mamuciam' derives from this location and translates as 'breast-shaped hill'. The site was chosen as a defensible location on a strategic hub of the routes between Roman settlements in York, Chester, Wigan, Ribchester and Middlewich. The fort went through several stages of development and was used right up until the end of the Roman occupation in AD 410. The reconstruction we see today is built on the original foundations and shows the fort as it would have looked in around AD 200.

Manchester Museum

The Manchester Museum collection started with the private collection of John Leigh Philips (1761–1814). In 1821, after his death, the Manchester Natural History Society was formed to take over the collection. In 1868 the collection was transferred to the University of Manchester, or Owens College as it was known at the time. They commissioned Alfred Waterhouse to design the magnificent Gothic structure we see today, and the museum was opened in 1890. It contains a wide range of exhibits and is particularly noted for its Egyptology collection.

St Ann's

Above: Built in a cornfield in 1712, when Manchester was just a small country village, St Ann's was only Manchester's second church, after what is now the cathedral. St Ann's Square was laid out in 1720 when Manchester was starting to grow as it headed into the Industrial Revolution.

St Peter's Square

Left: The square was originally the site of St Peter's Church, which stood here from 1788 to 1907. The Cenotaph was erected in 1924 to a design by Edward Lutyens and is a near replica of the one in London.